C000202220

Goa Paradise-on-Sea

NETS THROWN INTO THE DEEP SEA ARE RETURNED
OVERFLOWING WITH FISH.
PAGE 4: GENTLY SWAYING PALMS, LADEN WITH FRUIT,
STRETCHES OF SMOOTH GOLDEN SAND DISTURBED ONLY BY THE
FOOTSTEPS OF WOMEN WALKING OFF WITH BASKETS LADEN WITH
'FRUITS DE LA MER'.
PAGES 6-7: THE INTERIOR OF THE CHURCH OF ST. FRANCIS OF
ASSISI WITH ITS BAROQUE GILDED ALTAR AND THE TABERNACLE
IN A VAULTED NICHE AS THE CENTRAL FOCUS.

Goa Paradise-on-Sea

Annabel Lopez

Lustre Press
Roli Books

Historical Sketch of Goa

Goa, with its palm-fringed beaches, enchanting sunsets and *susegad* (easygoing) lifestyle has gained world renown as an irresistible tourist destination. Almost five centuries ago, the city of Goa was equally well known. The Portuguese had wrested Goa from its Muslim rulers and made it the capital of their empire in the east. Few then had not heard of Goa or were unaware of its location. Prior to the Portuguese, over a period of twenty centuries, Goa changed hands from Hindu to Muslim rulers quite a few times. If one were to go back even further, the origins of Goa are shrouded in myth and folklore.

Legend has it that the name Goa is derived from Goparashtra, a land of cowherds and nomadic tribes. The Hindu epic, Mahabharata, and the ancient Hindu text, *Harivansa*, refer to Goa as Gomant. The references show how the land originated or found favour with heavenly powers. In one reference, Parasurama, the sixth incarnation of Vishnu, shot an arrow from the summit of the Western Ghats into the Arabian Sea and commanded the waves to part. The spot where the arrow fell became his new kingdom, Gomant. In another reference, Parasurama after conquering Surparaka from the sea settled in Gomant with ten sages who had accompanied him from northern India. He then performed the most sacred of all sacrifices, the Asvamedha, at Haramal village in present-day Pernem *taluka* (a sub-district) for expiation of sins and attainment of celestial bliss . Yet another tale relates how the seven great sages or Sapta Rishis performed a penance for seven million years in Gomant and pleased the deity so much that he came to bless them in the form of Lord Shiva.

FACING PAGE: THE SE CATHEDRAL, OLD GOA, IS ASIA'S LARGEST CATHOLIC CATHEDRAL THAT CLOSELY FOLLOWED EUROPEAN CHURCH MODELS IN DESIGN AND DETAILING. BELOW: A ROCK-STREWN SANDY COVE SHELTERED BY A FRINGE OF COCONUT PALMS.

FACING PAGE: LUSH
GREEN PADDY FIELDS
AND TALL PALMS
AGAINST A BACKDROP
OF VERDANT HILL
SLOPES.

The romantic in me likes to narrate the tale of Lord Shiva taking temporary shelter in Gomant, under the name Gomantakesh, after deserting his wife and quitting his favourite abode in the snow-covered Himalaya. His devoted wife disguised herself as an *apsara* to follow him and won him over with her beauty and melodious voice.

Another not-so-romantic reference to Gomant is in the *Harivansa*. It is the place where a bloody battle was fought between Krishna and Jarasandha, which ended in the defeat of the king of Magadha in Central India.

EARLY INVADERS

Around 1500 B.C., the Aryans were the first to traverse the Indian peninsula and invade southern India. Natives and tribals driven from their land fled south as the Aryans advanced, leaving a trail of settlements of mixed creed and race. Habitation pockets in Goa, when the Aryans finally arrived around 600 B.C., are said to have comprised forest dwellers, hunters, gatherers of forest produce, and migratory cultivators.

Goa has also been mentioned in ancient Greek texts. But the earliest historical reference to Goa comes in 300 B.C. as part of the Mauryan Empire. The Mauryans conquered the Konkan and Emperor Ashoka renamed it Aparanta—Beyond The End. Many attempts were made to introduce Buddhism into the region, but the Hindu religion remained dominant.

HINDU RULERS

Over the next seven centuries, Hindu dynasties ruled over Goa. The Pallavas, Chalukyas, and Rashtrakutas dominated southern India; the Kadamba dynasty, an offshoot of the Pallavas, reigned supreme in Goa. It made Goa the capital of its empire, which comprised the southern Konkan region. In the latter half of the tenth century, the Kadambas ousted the Rashtrakutas from Chandrapura and subsequently shifted the seat of their empire to Govapuri (present-day Goa Velha).

Govapuri or Gopakkapattana was a deep natural harbour that boosted trade links with the Malabar Coast and Arabia. Huge sums poured in from consignments of horses and spices that passed through the port. Traders from across the seas, Arabs as well as East Africans, were warmly welcomed. Many settled down, building palatial houses and places of worship. Goa became noted for its opulence. It boasted of grand edifices, educational and charitable institutions, and some exquisite stone temples.

During the reign of King Jayakesi II, son-in-law of the great Chalukyan emperor Vikramaditya II, the inhabitants of Goa along with the rest of the Konkan rebelled against their rulers. The king's general, Sindavansa Mahamandleshvara Achugideva, suppressed the uprising, but the city was destroyed. A few years later, Sivachitta and Vishnuchitta, sons of King Jayakesi II, took over the reigns from their father and rebuilt the city of Goa.

MUSLIM INVADERS

The Kadamba temples, which housed the treasures of the kingdom, were the first targets of Muslim invaders. These raids led by Mahmud Ghazni of Delhi started as early as the tenth century. The Kadambas had an ally in the Chalukyas, which kept

the Muslim raiders at bay for the better part of the eleventh and twelfth centuries. With the death of the Chalukyan ruler in 1198, Goa lay vulnerable.

The Kadamba dynasty retained its hold over Goa till the middle of the thirteenth century, when the Yadavas of Devagiri took over Goa. In the late thirteenth century, Ala-ud-din's general, Malik Kafur, invaded southern India and captured Goa and other parts of Maharashtra. In the coming years, the inhabitants of Goa were in constant hostility with Malik Tubliga, in whose care Goa had been entrusted. The city was reduced to ruins.

In 1367, the Vijayanagara king, Harihara, ordered his general Madhavacharya Vidyaranya to oust the Muslims from Goa. The general was successful and even rebuilt the Sapta Koteshvara temple that the Muslims had destroyed.

Goa continued as a part of the kingdom of Vijayanagara till 1469. Then Mullek-ul-Tijur Khaje Jehan, a sultan of Mahomet II, the thirteenth Bahamani emperor, conquered it. The city fortified by towers and bulwarks was no match for a fleet of hundred and twenty ships assisted by land forces. It was forced to capitulate and was reduced to shambles.

This city, on the banks of the Zuari, was already facing decline as the river had silted and the harbour had become defunct. The Bahamanis moved further to the banks of the Mandovi, to an earlier religious centre of the Vijayanagara kingdom, and named the city Ela.

The Vijayanagara king tried to recapture the city in 1481, but failed miserably. After the death of the Bahamani king, Muhammad Shah II, Bahadur Khan Gillani seized power for a brief period before he was forced into submission. After the Bahamani dynasty left the scene in 1488, Goa fell into the hands of Prince Abdul Muzaffar Yussuf Adil Shah.

The Sultans of Bijapur turned Ela into a flourishing port for the trade of horses. The chief source of revenue was the custom duties levied on horses. As a result of its trade links, many eastern kingdoms maintained cordial ties with the rulers. The city was also the meeting ground for Muslim pilgrims who embarked there to proceed to Mecca. Being well-built and fortified, it attracted travellers who have admiringly described its beautiful edifices in travelogues. The most elegant buildings were the mosque and Adil Shah's fort palace overlooking

FACING PAGE: YOUNG BOYS AND GIRLS GAZE MESMERIZED OVER THE CANDLES IN THEIR HANDS DURING A FORMAL CHURCH SERVICE TO CELEBRATE THEIR FIRST HOLY COMMUNION. BELOW: A MUSICIAN PRACTISES HIS VIOLIN AS HE WATCHES THE WORLD GO BY FROM THE WINDOW OF HIS PORTUGUESE COLONIAL MANSION.

FISHER FOLK SCOUR THE SAND FOR SHELLFISH
THAT BURROW DEEP INTO THE WET SAND.

the Mandovi. The palace has been described as having large elegant halls opening onto colonnaded porches and carved wooden columns.

The private residences of the people were also fairly large but single storeyed. Bazaars abounded with shops of traders and craftsmen. The goldsmiths, in particular, were renowned as the best in the country. There were also many public buildings.

ARRIVAL OF THE PORTUGUESE

Portuguese navigator Vasco da Gama sailed down the Malabar Coast in 1498, and twelve years later, Alfonso Albuquerque, who had a powerful fleet, conceived of a plan to found a vast empire in the East with Goa as its capital. Goa, situated on the west coast of India, commanded a favourable position for trade with Asia, had two splendid harbours and an exemplary naval station. It appeared to suit Albuquerque's requirements.

Goa itself was an easy prey for invaders. The local populace had grown tired of tyrannical Muslim rulers. In February 1510, Alfonso de Albuquerque with twenty ships, a few smaller vessels and 1,200 men, took over the city without resistance. Albuquerque, pleased with the easy conquest, showed immense mercy towards his new subjects. He issued a proclamation that equal justice and protection be extended to all the new subjects of the King of Portugal. He forbade his soldiers from plundering, looting or harassing the natives at his defeat.

Adil Shah, taken by surprise, made strenuous efforts to regain Goa. With the support of the native Muslims, three months after its capture on 23 May 1510, Adil Shah laid siege to the city and re-conquered it with the help of 60,000 men.

With the onset of the monsoons, Albuquerque was forced to take refuge in his fleet of ships just off Panaji. After four months on the ships, where his men only had basic provisions, they sailed to Cannanore and made preparations to lay siege, a second time on 24 November 1510. A bloody battle saw 2,000 Muslims die, while the Portuguese lost a mere forty men. Victorious, Albuquerque entered the city with the royal flag flying high. This time round, livid with the Muslims, he ordered their massacre. His soldiers plundered the city and subjected the people to unimaginable cruelties. Fearing a re-conquest, Albuquerque began the arduous task of rebuilding the city of Goa.

Albuquerque was as accomplished a statesman as he was a general. Goa's golden era began under his rule. He made every effort to safeguard his new empire. His subjects were kept happy by a just and fair legislative system. The taxes imposed were as low as possible.

THE RETABLE OF THE ALTAR OF SE CATHEDRAL, THE THEME OF WHICH IS THE LIFE AND TRIUMPH OF ST. CATHERINE OF ALEXANDRIA. ON HER FEAST DAY, NOVEMBER 25, GOA WAS CONQUERED BY THE PORTUGUESE FROM THE SULTAN OF BIJAPUR.

Albuquerque set up the first municipality, consisting only of the inhabitants. A judicial system was also set up, and funds were set aside for the destitute. The inhabitants of Goa enjoyed administrative privileges at par with the people of Lisbon. The senate and the municipal council had direct communication with the king of Portugal. A special representative looked after Goa's interests in court.

Muslims were, however, treated harshly; Hindus were favoured and allowed to carry on all their religious practices barring *sati*. Albuquerque also strove to bridge the gap between the rulers and the native population. He actively encouraged intermarriages and bestowed the newly-weds with gifts and property confiscated from the Muslims.

After the death of Alfonso de Albuquerque in 1515, the city continued to grow in size and grandeur. Architecture developed. Buildings, both private residences and public institutions, were built on every vacant plot. In 1540, Goa accommodated 2,00,000 people.

GOA DOURADA

It was around 1560-70 that Goa was the Rome of the East, its golden era at its height. The Portuguese used Goa, ideally located at the centre of Asia's most prosperous trade route, as their base for operations along the Malabar Coast. They made huge profits from the trade of Arabian horses to the subcontinent and shipments of spices to Europe. Wealth that poured into the government's coffers, from taxes imposed on goods that passed through its ports, built the city.

Accounts of travellers who visited the city reveal its ostentation. One traveller recounted:

> 'The hills were surmounted with elegant structures. Churches and convents towered high into the sky, while lower down the hillsides were magnificent palaces. The city was a maze of numerous streets, squares, public institutions, and private houses. The suburbs were densely populated with villas and meandering walkways. The banks of the river were considered prime location[s] and the villas were seated in wooded compounds of palm groves and fruit laden orchards.'

DECLINE OF THE CITY

Economic and natural factors led to the city's decline. Disaster struck in 1543 when a virulent strain of cholera broke out and overwhelmed the city, killing hundreds each day. Even pets and farm animals fell victim to it.

The city, being amid a marshy swamp, was an ideal breeding ground for mosquitoes. Malaria spread like wild fire. Human waste was carelessly discharged; no system was in place for disposal. Pure, drinking water was in short supply. Poor drainage caused wells, the only source of drinking water, to get infected by raw sewage. This, in turn, encouraged germs and diseases.

FACING PAGE:
CARVED ROSEWOOD
FURNITURE, BELGIAN
GLASS CHANDELIERS
AND ITALIAN MOSAIC
TILES GIVE AN
EXOTIC LOOK TO THE
MANSION.

Around 1570, the Muslim rulers of the Deccan joined hands to try and wrest Goa away from the Portuguese. They were forced to retreat after ten months of a fruitless siege. The resultant famine and an epidemic fever in 1570 wiped out nearly fifty per cent of the city's population. After the epidemic the city picked up the threads and began showing signs of revival and constructive enthusiasm. New buildings came up and by the end of the sixteenth century, nearly 2,500 new immigrants were coming in every year, replenishing the population.

As opulence grew, decadence stepped up. Adultery, drunkenness, and prostitution were rife among the Portuguese and a large section of the local population, especially, the landed gentry.

Another important factor that led to the downfall of the city was the silting up of the Mandovi. Ships could no longer enter the harbour. Moreover, Portugal's trade monopoly was taken over by the British, French, and Dutch.

In 1603, when Viceroy Ayres de Saldanha governed Goa, the Dutch made a futile attempt at conquering it. Their trade links in the east strengthened much to the annoyance of the Portuguese. Goa's golden era began to pall. The Dutch laid siege to the harbour again in 1643, when they captured Ceylon, Malacca, and the Moluccas from the Portuguese, further reducing Portugal's trade. The effects were immediately visible. Those once affluent were forced to live off alms. The population deteriorated though Goa was still an important place on the map of the East.

THE MARATHA STRENGTH

The Marathas led by Shivaji constantly challenged the mighty Moghul power. In 1664, they took Surat from the Mughals. The Marathas then attacked Chaul, a Portuguese post, and later, took over Bassein and Salcete in 1737. They, however, accepted defeat before attempting an attack on the capital city and signed a treaty in May 1739, whereby they withdrew entirely from Goa in exchange for Portugal's northern territories like Bassein, but not Daman.

NEW CONQUESTS AND THE EMERGENCE OF PANAJI

After the city's decline, there was a move to shift the capital to Mormugao, another natural harbour. But the plan was abandoned in 1707 and the capital then shifted to Panaji, further upstream.

The damage to the once-beautiful city of Goa was done. Houses were left behind and became dilapidated. Some were pulled down to provide building material for the new capital. The palaces and country mansions disappeared. All that remained were a few convents and churches.

The population of Old Goa had slumped by this time but that of the adjoining provinces of Margao and Mapusa had increased. With the loss of territories to the north of Goa, the Portuguese looked at extending their foothold in other strategic places between 1780 and 1790. They annexed neighbouring Bicholim, Sattari, and Pernem. In 1791, Ponda along with Sanguem, Quepem, and Canacona in south Goa were added to the Portuguese empire.

At the beginning of the nineteenth century, Panaji was a sleepy fishing village with a few hundred houses and a crumbling fort. Although it had a handful of churches

BIRDS, PLOVERS AND
TERNS APPEAR
DAZZLED BY THE
EXPANSE OF THE
OPEN SEA
AND THE BRIGHT
AFTERNOON SUN.
PAGES 22-23:
STREET DANCES AND
CULTURAL FUNCTIONS
BREAK ALL BARRIERS
AND ARE OCCASIONS
WHEN THE YOUNG
AND THE OLD, THE
RICH AND THE POOR,
ALL ENJOY
THEMSELVES.

and chapels, the summer palace of Adil Shah on the waterfront was *the* building. Now, sand dunes were flattened, swamps drained, and land reclaimed to build the new capital. Panaji gained in importance, as the viceroy shifted his residence to it. It was declared the capital of Portuguese India in 1843. The city grew in size while elsewhere the first seeds of a freedom struggle were being sowed.

LIBERATION MOVEMENT

In 1824, the reigning Queen of Portugal, Maria II, sought to placate the Goans: she offered the post of governor to a local. The ploy failed and mounting uprisings led to a couple of coups and mutinies, the worst of which was the massacre of Gaspar Dias in 1835. The whole regiment in the fort was slain. The Portuguese, however, continued in power.

It was the Hindu faction in Goa that was unhappy with Portuguese rule. Their treatment as second-class citizens kept off high government postings had strengthened their motivation. They led the freedom struggle.

When Salazar took over as Portugal's dictator, he faced immense pressure to relinquish his hold on Goa. The issue was brought to the fore once the British withdrew from India in 1947. The Portuguese government, however, showed no signs of relenting and Prime Minister Jawaharlal Nehru sent in armed forces to liberate the Goans from 450 years of colonial rule. The liberation offensive, Operation Vijay, met with little resistance from the Portuguese and the three territories of Goa, Daman, and Diu were handed over to the Indian Government. Goa was made into a Union Territory with its own government.

RECENT HISTORY

Political upheavals have dogged the union territory of Goa. It was declared a full-fledged state of the Indian Union in 1987. The state has, however, seen little progress or development thanks to frequent changes of government. While the Congress has found a majority in the legislative assembly for most of Goa's political life, the Bharatiya Janata Party has emerged as the stronger force.

Religious Fervour

FACING PAGE: THE FEAST OF EACH CHURCH IS CELEBRATED WITH GREAT POMP AND SOLEMNITY.

Places of worship have drawn a great deal of attention since time immemorial. In civilisations across the globe, sacred shrines are invariably, unique architectural marvels.

From the surviving examples of temple art, we deduce that Goa was no different. The plains around the trading port of Goa boasted of the most exquisite temples. The revenue from trade and the income from fertile agricultural land assured that financial resources were available for building abodes for the gods. In contrast, the hinterlands of Goa and the hilly terrain beyond, which generated hardly any revenue, did not have any temples to be proud off.

The earliest traces of religious architecture belong to the period between 5th and 10th century A.D. Based on the inscription found at site, the rock-cut caves at Arvalem in Bicholim *taluka*, dedicated to Lord Shiva are early fifth century. Fragments belonging to Hindu temples, like the Vahana, the vehicle of Lord Shiva, found by Father Heras in Chandor, have been dated to seventh century A.D. The Shiva temple in Chandor, built of bricks, is the oldest structural Hindu temple in Goa.

The period after the tenth century A.D., under the reign of the Kadamba dynasty, probably had the most elaborate temples, judging from the large number of fragments of temple art that have been attributed to this period. Despite the abundance of laterite in the region, it appears that basalt was the preferred building material. Perhaps the stone, though rare in this belt, was preferred because it allowed intricate relief carvings unlike the very brittle laterite. The many fragments of basalt carvings housed in the museum at the Pilar seminary are evidence of the intricacy of the temples of the period. Samples of intricate carvings can also be seen at the State Archaeological Museum at Panaji and the museum installed in the Convent of St. Francis of Assisi in Old Goa.

WAR OF RELIGIONS

The nature and symbolism of the structure also meant that these abodes of the heavenly powers were the first to be targeted when invaders laid siege to the place. Temples of the original Hindu inhabitants were destroyed by Muslim dynasties that conquered Goa in the 14th and 15th centuries. The religious harmony that allowed both Hinduism and Islam to coexist till this point disappeared with the arrival of the Bahamani rulers. Even the sacred nature of religious edifices did not spare them from destruction. All, except the exquisite stone-carved Shiva shrine at Tambdi Surla, of the Kadamba period, were razed to the ground. Built entirely out of basalt this temple is dated circa A.D. 13.

Portuguese domination and the spread of Christianity characterize the sixteenth century in the history of Goa. The day the Portuguese seized the city for the second time, 25 November 1510, is dedicated to the memory of the martyr, St. Catherine of Alexandria. The Portuguese immediately raised a chapel, close to the landing place, in her honour and chose her as the patroness of the city. The chapel still exists today, though it must have seen a number of renovations over the years.

The Portuguese, having seized the trading port from the Muslims, systematically went about destroying all Muslim places of worship. The lone Muslim survivor is the Safa Shahouri Masjid just outside Ponda, which the Bijapuri ruler, Adil Shah, had built in 1560. The whitewashed walls and sloping terracotta roof, however, characterise later additions.

After Portugal established their trade links in the east, they directed their attention towards the propagation of Christianity. The government encouraged missionaries from various religious orders to set up residences in the newly conquered territory. Partly by force and partly by coercion, these missionaries carried out their work of conversion.

SPREAD OF CHRISTIANITY

The **Franciscans** were the first to arrive in Goa and had the honour of being the first pastors in the newly conquered territory. They first built the convent of St. Francis of Assisi, which was subsequently rebuilt and then a church adjoining it in 1521. The church, rebuilt in 1661, has a Tuscan facade, an Indo-Baroque interior and a Manueline-style doorway saved from the first church. The interior is rib vaulted and decorated with bold floral frescoes. There is an interesting carved floral pulpit, gilded main altar and a floor that appears almost paved with inscribed tombstones. Especially noteworthy are the seventeenth-century wall paintings as are the paintings on the life of St. Francis.

Goa was given the status of a Bishopric in 1534. Three years later, Father John of Albuquerque, a Franciscan priest, was made the first Bishop of Goa. The seminary of the Holy Faith (Santa Fe) was established in 1541 by two secular priests, Michael Vaz and James Borba, for the newly converted population.

After the Franciscans, the next to arrive were the **Dominicans,** who maintained a low profile till about 1560. They built the Church of Our Lady of the Rosary, which was converted into a parochial church during the epidemics that hit the city of Goa. In 1548, they built their own convent and church.

Given the humble stature of the first chapel, dedicated to St. Catherine, Portuguese Viceroy Dom Francisco Coutinho, Count of Redondo (1561–64), was instructed by the Portuguese government to commission 'a grandiose church worthy of the wealth, power and fame of the Portuguese.' The church, built as a result, came to be known as Se Cathedral and is the largest in Asia.

Engineers Julio Simao and Antonio Argueiros, were responsible for this west-facing cathedral with a Tuscan exterior and square towers in the Manueline style. One surviving tower houses the golden bell. The largest bell in Asia, it was cast in Cuncolim, a village in south Goa. It tolled during the infamous Inquisition to announce the start of the gruesome *Auto da fe* or Acts of Faith, when suspected heretics were dragged out of the Palace of Inquisition's dungeons across the square.

The intricately detailed Corinthian interior has huge pillars dividing the 76.2 metre-long central space from the side aisles. The cathedral has as many as fifteen altars dedicated to Our Ladies of Hope, Anguish and Three Needs among others and a grand altar dedicated to St. Catherine of Alexandria. The gilded, ornate main altar has nine carved frames and a magnificent crucifix. The life of St. Catherine of Alexandria is depicted on the panels. Some of the visuals are of her interaction with the Roman emperor Maxim and her flogging and martyrdom.

The chapels of the Blessed Sacrament and the Cross of Miracles (perpetually growing wooden cross) have exquisite filigree work on the screens. The cross was originally in a village church till a

THE FORT OF TIRACOL, WHICH GUARDS THE ESTUARY AT THE NORTHERN TIP OF TIRACOL, HAS IN ITS COBBLED COURTYARD A CHAPEL DEDICATED TO ST. ANTHONY AND A STATUE OF CHRIST.

A HOLY CROSS ATOP THE HILL OVERLOOKING
ARAMBOL BEACH.

TOP: THOUSANDS OF PILGRIMS MAKE THEIR WAY TO OLD GOA DURING THE EXPOSITIONS TO PAY HOMAGE TO THEIR PATRON SAINT.
LEFT: VOICES BOOMING TO THE ACCOMPANIMENT OF THE GUITAR SING OUT PRAISES TO THE LORD.

A STATUE OF THE
MADONNA WITH A
SERENE AND MELLOW
EXPRESSION, ADORNING
AN ALTAR RETABLE.

THE SACRED
TULSI PLANT IN ITS
COLOURFUL PLANTER,
IN FRONT OF WHICH A
DEVOTEE PERFORMS AN
AARTI AND MAKES AN
OFFERING OF FLOWERS.

vision of Christ is said to have appeared on it. It is now in a box with a little aperture to allow pilgrims to touch it.

For all practical purposes, the **Jesuits** were the second order to settle in Goa and organize themselves into a community. The legendary Jesuit missionary, Francis Xavier, arrived in Goa in 1542 with Governor Alfonso Martin de Sousa. Francis Xavier is reputed to have converted hundreds of people. He was also responsible for bringing errant sheep back into the fold of the church. Debauched and immoral Portuguese officers were persuaded to become regular churchgoers and partake in the sacraments.

In 1543, Santa Fe was handed over to the Jesuits who changed its name to the College of St. Paul. As a result of its popularity, the Jesuits began to be known as Paulists or as Apostles. They became the chief apostolic preachers in the east

Under the aegis of the Jesuits, an order was passed to close all Hindu houses of worship and ban idol worship. Brahmin priests were exiled. As the fervour of conversions increased, temples were razed to the ground and mass conversions carried out. In 1546, King John III passed a decree that all converted Christians be granted the same privileges, offices and liberties that were up to then reserved for the Portuguese. Credit for this can perhaps be given to Francis Xavier.

The Inquisition, with its bloody trials and *Auto da fes* or Acts of Faith was established in 1560 under the administration of Viceroy Constantine de Braganza. Any one who deviated from the Catholic Church was imprisoned in the dungeons of the Inquisition headquarters and subjected to appalling torture.

BASCILICA DE BOM JESUS

Goa's most important church is dedicated to the Infant Jesus and was built by the Jesuits. Construction commenced in 1594 and was completed in 1605. Columns of the Doric, Corinthian and Composite order and intricately carved basalt embellishments make its facade one of the richest in Goa. The four-storeyed facade has no towers flanking it, but a single tower has been placed at the eastern end.

The layout of the church follows simplistic Renaissance norms, while the detailing and decoration is Baroque. A statue of St. Ignatius of Loyola is placed above the elaborately carved and gilded altar that also has the infant Jesus.

A Florentine sculptor, Giovanni Batista Foggini, made the tomb of St. Francis Xavier. It was a present from the last Medici, the Duke of Tuscany, Cosimo III.

Having taken ten years to build, the tomb with three tiers in marble carvings and jasper, was assembled in 1698. The sacred relics of St. Francis Xavier, contained in a silver casket within the tomb, draw religious pilgrims from all over the world.

The **Augustinians,** being the fourth order to arrive in Goa, commenced construction of their monastery in 1572. The grand interior had eight chapels, four altars, Persian-tile-relief sculpture and murals. The tower, which is all that remains of the five-story high facade, soars up 46 metres into the sky.

The **Carmelites** established their convent in Goa in 1607. An offshoot of this order established a convent in Chimbel for the second caste in Goa, the *Chardos* or Khatrias.

The **Theatines** arrived in Goa in the middle of the seventeenth century and built a church modelled on St. Peter's, Rome, between 1656 and 1700. The three-storeyed facade has Corinthian columns and pilasters of giant proportions. It is shaped in the Greek cross plan with a semicircular apse. Above the centre of the nave is a dome, resting on a drum topped with a cupola. The baroque interior is ornamented with gilded altars, rare paintings and stucco decorations on the walls.

Up to 1542, the Se was the only parochial church in the city of Goa, but by 1548, Christianity had spread to all corners of the city, to the island of Goa and even to the smaller neighbouring islands and the mainland. By 1557, Goa was raised to an Archbishopric and Primary of the East Indies. In 1560, D. Gaspar de Leon Pereira was consecrated the first Archbishop of Goa. Christianity spread south to Salcete, and within fifty years almost 28 churches were built all over Salcete.

What remains of the grand City of Goa today is a mere shadow of a city that once had grand houses, crowded bazaars, a buzzing quayside, elegant shops and office buildings. Rua Direita was the main Business Street of sixteenth-century Old Goa. There is, however, no trace of either the street or the residential and commercial buildings of the city. In the overgrown jungle that covers the City of Goa all that remains are churches, convents and monasteries. The three big churches—Bascilica de Bom Jesus, Se Cathedral and the Church and Convent of St. Francis of Assisi—cluster in one group. The Convent houses a museum maintained by the Archaeological Survey of India. Close to the Church and Convent of St. Francis of Assisi are the Chapel of St. Catherine (1510) and the ruins of the Palace of the Inquisition. A stone's throw from the quayside is the Viceroy's arch, designed by Julio

THE PAGEANT ON THE OCCASION OF THE FEAST OF 'THREE KINGS', WHEN THREE BOYS FROM A VILLAGE DRESS UP AS KINGS.

PRIESTS ARE THE
CARETAKERS OF THE
TEMPLE AND ALSO
FUNCTION AS THE CHIEF
EXECUTORS OF THE
DEITY'S COMMANDS.

Simao, originally built by Francis da Gama (Viceroy, 1597–1600) and subsequently rebuilt in 1954.

East of the Viceroy's arch is the Church of St. Cajetan and the Gate of the Palace of Adil Shah. What was formerly Adil Shah's principal palace was used as the Viceroy's residence from 1554–1695 with the Tronco Prison in one wing.

HINDU ENCLAVES

Dotting the lush green forests around Ponda are two clusters of Hindu temples built during the seventeenth and eighteenth centuries. To counteract the harsh treatment being meted out by the Portuguese during the Old conquests, the few remaining Hindu families fled with their deities to the hinterland, which was still a Christian-free haven, and built new structures to house these deities.

Over the years, the temples have expanded and metamorphosed. We now have these fairly modern temples with deities that have been venerated for centuries. They still draw devotees, descendants of the original families, who come to seek the deity's blessings before an auspicious moment in their lives. The most distinctive Goan feature in these temples is the lamp tower.

The first cluster of temples is north of Ponda, on the highway from Panaji. The most important of these is the Shiva temple of Shri Manguesh between villages Mardol and Priol. The original deity was housed in Cortalim and brought to the present location around the sixteenth century. The complex has a courtyard with a water tank and a stunning seven-storeyed *deepmal* or oil-lamp tower. The present temple, circa eighteenth century is a white building raised on a plinth. The marbled interior has decorative tiles on the wall and the silver embossed door to the inner sanctum, which houses the Shiva *lingam,* is flanked by two *dwarpalas.*

A little further down the road is the Sri Mahalsa temple dedicated to Vishnu. It was brought here in the seventeenth century from its location in present-day Salcete *taluka.* The most exceptional feature of this temple is its 12-tiered *deepmal.* The *deepmal* stands atop a *Kurma,* the tortoise incarnation of Lord Vishnu. Also noteworthy is the wooden *mandapa* with a marble floor and carved pillars. The elaborate carving on the ceiling has parakeet motifs, while that of the eaves depicts the various incarnations of Lord Vishnu.

A second cluster of temples is found deep in the countryside just outside Ponda. These are the Sri Ramnath, Shri Manguesh and the Shri Shanta Durga temples. The

BOTH IN INSPIRATION
AND DESIGN, CHURCHES
ARE THE SPIRITUAL
AND ARCHITECTURAL
CENTRES OF THE
VILLAGE THEY
STAND IN.

FACING PAGE: INTERIOR
OF SE CATHEDRAL
WHERE THE *PIECE DE
RESISTANCE* IS THE
GILDED HIGH ALTAR,
DEPICTING SCENES
FROM THE LIFE OF ST.
CATHERINE OF
ALEXANDRIA.
PAGES 38-39: GOA'S
SPLENDID BEACHES
STRETCH OVER 106 KM
OF COASTLINE, FROM
QUERIM IN THE NORTH
TO MOBOR IN THE
SOUTH.

Shanta Durga temple, dedicated to the Goddess of Peace, is an unusual pagoda-like structure with a roof of stone slabs. It is in a breathtaking clearing in a green forest at Kavalem. The original temple that was at this site was more than 400 years old. Shahu, grandson of the great Maratha ruler, Shivaji, erected this temple in 1738. Within the temple complex is the obligatory tank for ablutions and a five-storeyed *deepmal*. Glittering chandeliers are suspended from the elaborate ceiling in the large hall and silver embossed screens enclose the sanctuary. The silver image of the deity—an incarnation of Shiva's consort, Parvati—is enshrined inside the sanctuary. The *raths* (chariots) are used during the *jatra*, held in January.

A stone's throw from this temple is that of Sri Ramnath. The *lingam*, worshipped by devotees of Lords Shiva and Vishnu, was brought to this location from the village of Loutolim. A noteworthy feature in this temple is a silver screen in the inner sanctum that is embossed with animal and floral motifs.

North Goa is dotted with ancient temples, a reminder of the thriving Hindu population. The Bhagavati temple in Pernem is on a 500-year-old site, though what is seen today is an eighteenth-century structure. It is dedicated to the eight-armed Bhagavati, an incarnation of Goddess Parvati. The magnificent gateway is framed by two life-size elephants.

Of the newer temples, the Mahalaxmi temple in Panaji attracts throngs of devotees who come to touch the feet of the deity and receive blessings.

The three religions in Goa present a fusion of cultures seldom found anywhere else in the world. The houses of worship, be it the churches built by the Portuguese, the temples around Ponda or mosques, are architectural marvels that display a unique symbiosis. It is only in Goa that one has chandeliers oscillating in Hindu temples, sloping roofs over mosques and Hindu motifs adorning Christian altars.

Essence of Goa

The first rays of the sun peeping over the horizon, tingeing the sky a delicate pink . . . soft white sand, patterned by sand crabs, still cool beneath bare feet . . . frothy waves crashing onto the beach and further afield, a school of dolphins pirouetting in the waters. Even as you watch, fishing boats can be seen bobbing on the water, heading home with the day's catch. Seagulls circle the skies in anticipation. The air is soon resounding with the rhythmic cries of fishermen, as a collected effort is made to drag the boat in and empty the catch on the pristine white sand. The beach is alive; the day's activity has commenced. Nothing prepares you for the buzzing crowds as the sun rises higher into the sky and buses empty their first load of tourists. Beach shacks that downed their palm-frond shutters well past midnight are preparing for their breakfast customers. Hawkers and hair 'braiders' walk along the shore looking for prey.

FACING PAGE: GOA HAS ALWAYS BEEN A HAVEN FOR BACKPACKERS AND HIPPIES. IN THE RECENT YEARS IT HAS GAINED WORLD RENOWN FOR ITS FULL-MOON RAVE PARTIES AND FLEA MARKETS.

These are images that can be used to describe any of the beaches in Goa. Some are crowded and pulsing with life; others are relatively quiet and peaceful. There are many to choose from. The beaches are, of course, Goa's much-talked-about feature. But, Goa's geography is varied and has more to offer.

A small tropical paradise, Goa, covers approximately 3,701 sq km. It has a 105-km coastline from north to south, while its width is just 65 km. The state of Maharashtra lies to its north; Karnataka is to its south.

To the east of Goa is the richly forested Sahyadri mountain range, a natural barrier separating Goa from the rest of the country. These Western Ghats are the least known part of Goa. They are rich reservoirs of biodiversity with a bewildering range of plant and animal life and provide a variety of raw products. The hills are the natural catchment areas for rain, protected as they are by a dense forest cover. There are a smattering of communities, comprising scheduled castes and tribes, who live off the produce of the forests and the cultivable land as did their ancestors many centuries ago.

The highest peak in Goa is the Sonsagar at 1,166 m / 3,827 ft from which rises the famous Dudhsagar (*dudh*: milk; *sagar*: ocean) fall. The Dudhsagar is a mere trickle in the dry season. It swells during the monsoon, falling over the cliff in the milk-white fury that gives the fall its name.

The gentle hills with rolling hillsides and slopes melt into the alluvial plains, which form Goa's midland. This is Goa's most densely populated region and for all practical purposes, the heartland of Goa. It is a fertile inland strip that has been carved out into a mosaic of paddy fields irrigated by rivers. It gives Goa two crops every year. The lush picturesque countryside is dotted with villages.

Goa's famous coastline stretches for just over a hundred kilometres. Each beach is different in its sameness. Clumps of coconut palms in swaying rows and endless sand dunes line the beaches creating a panoramic vista.

CLIMATE

Goa's is a warm tropical climate. The dry spell lasts for eight months, from October to May, when the days are warm and sunny, with temperatures hovering between 30-33 degrees centigrade. The humidity rises during the peak summer months, March to April. The monsoon is the most glorious season. Goa lies in the path of the south-

west monsoon and come June, it is deluge time. The small state receives roughly 90 inches of rain yearly.

The first two weeks of rain cover Goa in a moss green carpet, which within a few weeks, yields into lush, dark shrubbery. Whole villages get marooned once the roads flood. If the rain holds till August, the rice grown in early June has good prospects.

The months immediately before the monsoon witness high activity—the whole place has to gear up for the rains. Fields are weeded and prepared for planting. Roofs are repaired, palm frond awnings put up to protect verandas, balconies, doors and windows. The fishing grinds to a halt, as the sea is too turbulent for the fishing

THE HIGH TIDE OF TOURISM FLOODS GOA FROM OCTOBER TO MARCH WHEN SUN SEEKERS, MOSTLY EUROPEANS AND AMERICANS, MORE THAN DOUBLE THE POPULATION OF BEACH TOWNS.

boats. The boats are docked in sheds, and the fishing gear packed away. The women get ready for a lean season, when dried salt fish will have to be eaten in the absence of the fresh catch.

RIVERS

The rivers drain out the monsoon water trapped in the hilly areas into the sea. All the rivers in Goa are tidal rivers for quite a distance. In some, the ebb and flow of the tides is felt up to a distance of 30–40 metres inland. The salinity of the rivers and of the wells along their banks varies from the monsoon to the non-monsoon seasons.

From the natural eastern boundary of Goa rise two of its major rivers, the Mandovi and Zuari. They create a network of estuaries as they flow westwards to the Arabian Sea. The Mandovi traverses 81 km, while the Zuari covers 67 km, before plunging into the sea, creating a deep natural harbour, the Mormugao. The Mandovi widens out leaving in its wake picturesque little islands like Chorao, Divar, Zua and Cumbarjua. A network of tributaries from these two rivers fans out, covering most of Goa. Chapora river in the north and the Sal, Talpona, and Galibaga rivers in the south cover regions left untouched by the Mandovi and Zuari. The Tiracol river, the northern boundary of Goa, passes through the state for a mere 27.5 km. It then empties into the Arabian Sea.

BIODIVERSITY

Goa is enriched with a fascinating diversity of wildlife. It is estimated that Goa harbours 48 genera of mammals, 275 genera of birds and 60 genera of reptiles. The species from the cat family seen occasionally in Goa are the leopard, toddy cat, jungle cat, and the small Indian civet. The common mongoose is seen frequently near settlements. The jackal, striped hyena, and wild dog can be seen even during the day.

A special treat is glimpsing the common otter and the smooth Indian otter at water ponds. Quite a few varieties of bats are found in Goa—the Fulvous fruit bat, Rufus horseshoe bat, Dormer's bat and the Malay false vampire. Flying foxes and short-nosed fruit bats are encountered around dusk. Another forest creature here is the squirrel. The Indian giant squirrel is fairly common, as are the three-striped palm squirrel, the five-striped palm squirrel and the common brown giant flying squirrel.

Belonging to the rodent family is the Indian field mouse, the common house rat, the Indian Gerbille and Bandicoot—all found in plenty. Another creature that destroys plants is the common Indian porcupine of the forests. The hare resides on the grassy hillsides while a variety of antelopes like the sambar, *cheetal*, barking deer,

TWO GENERATIONS MAY LOOK DIFFERENT YET THEY SHARE THE SAME GOAN VALUES—GOOD CHEER, WARMTH, AND HOSPITALITY.
FACING PAGE: FREE SPIRITS THRONG THE BEACHES DURING PEAK SEASON.

mouse deer, and hog deer are forest dwellers. The wild boar, farmers' enemy since it damages crops, is seen in orchards and cashew plantations. Other important mammalian species include the bison, ox, monkey (Bonnet Macaque, and common langur) and Indian elephant. Sea mammals include the sea cow, porpoise and long-beaked dolphin.

Goa has three wildlife sanctuaries and a bird sanctuary noted for their scenic beauty and large tracts of wilderness with a variety of plant and animal life. Along the north-east border of Goa, at Molem, is the Bhagwan Mahavir wildlife sanctuary. Covering an area of 240 sq km, it is the biggest of the three sanctuaries in Goa. In its thick forest-clad slopes and verdant valleys, the slender Loris is occasionally found. It is also a paradise for bird watchers. Bondla forest, 50 km from Panaji, has a mini-zoo, a sprawling deer park a botanical garden and a rose garden. The Cotigao wildlife sanctuary is the second largest with an area of 105 sq km and is 50 km off Margao in South Goa. It is covered with dense forests and has varied wildlife, avian fauna, and reptiles. The sloth bear has on rare occasions been sighted there.

The Salim Ali bird sanctuary in Chorao is spread over 1.78 sq km and is at the western tip of the island of Chorao along the Mandovi river near Panaji. It is fully covered with mangrove species. Many varieties of local, as well as migratory birds frequent the area. The common birds are: the little, median and cattle egret, cormorant, coot, openbill stork, kingfisher, drongo, bulbul, weaverbird, dove, parrot, vulture, kite, quail, and hoopoe.

The dense forests which receive heavy rainfall are excellent natural habitats for snakes and other reptiles. The non-poisonous snakes found in Goa are the common blind snake, Russell's sand boa, Indian python, Indian wart snake, trinket snake, and the Indian rat snake. Other varieties of non-poisonous snakes, like the gerdon, golden tree snake, common wolf snake, chequered keelback, striped keelback, Indian gamma, and the common green whip snake are seen occasionally. The poisonous snakes commonly found are the Indian cobra, common Indian krait, Russell's viper, saw scaled viper, and the bamboo pit viper.

Turtles are fairly common. They are found in wells, streams, and paddy fields, especially, during the monsoon. The sea turtle that comes to the shore to lay eggs is facing extinction: its eggs are a much-sought-after delicacy. A few crocodiles have been sighted in the Cumbarjua canal, which has become a popular tourist spot. Another reptile, the monitor lizard, is facing extinction since it is caught when sighted and devoured.

ECONOMY

The mining industry makes up a large chunk of Goa's economy. Goa has been exporting its rich, natural resources of iron ore, manganese, and bauxite to Japan and Korea. The Mandovi and Zuari, along with their tributaries, act as a natural transport network for the ore. Barges carry the ore from mines in the hinterland to the port at Mormugao, where it is loaded onto cargo ships. A couple of Hindu families controlled the mining industry. They had the foresight to buy large tracts a couple of generations ago. The present generations are still reaping the benefits.

STRIKING A BARGAIN AT ANJUNA'S WEEKLY FLEA MARKET.

TOURISM

It remains Goa's biggest money-spinner. Foreign tourists were lured into Goa as early as the 1960s. Besides the famous beaches, Goa's cheap food, easily available accommodation and soft stance on drugs, nudity and drink attracted tourists. The beaches around Calangute were a haven for hippies. An influx of backpackers made Goa synonymous with hippies and drug trafficking. In the '80s, tourism took off. International charters from Europe brought planeloads of holidaymakers for week-long package holidays. The beach stretch from Calangute to Vagator saw hundreds of hotels mushroom up almost overnight. With the hotels came taxis, beach shacks, souvenir shops . . . Today, tourism is an emotional and sensitive subject, with equal arguments for and against it.

AGRICULTURE

Farming is a major occupation. The fertile alluvial soil of Goa coupled with a warm, tropical climate allows a variety of crops. Two cycles of paddy growing produce rice, the staple diet. Goa also abounds in vegetables like ladyfinger, brinjal, pumpkin and gourd.

The hillsides are used optimally. Cashew and bamboo plantations are restricted to the upper reaches of the slopes. The lower parts are used for areca nut horticultural plantations, having a multiple cropping system. The plants cultivated using this system are pepper, cardamom, mango, jackfruit, pineapple, cashew and *jamun*.

The low coastal region has coconut groves. Besides being an icon that immediately paints picturesque images of a beach, the coconut palm is a versatile plant. Almost every part of the palm is put to some use. The trunk is used for construction, mainly for roofs of houses. The fronds are made into awnings to protect houses from the fury of the monsoon; the sticks of the leaves turn into brooms. Whatever does not get used is burnt as firewood.

The raw coconut is split open to provide a refreshing drink, while the kernel of the ripe coconut is used in almost every Goan dish. Oil is extracted from the dried kernel, which is used in the manufacture of soap and as a cooking medium. Toddy is tapped from tender young shoots and is used to make *feni*, jaggery or vinegar. Tender palm fronds are eaten either raw or cooked as a vegetable and relished as a delicacy.

The coconut is de-husked before breaking it for the kernel. The fibrous husk is used to make a number of items of commercial value, ranging from coir rope, mattresses and fishing nets to doormats.

CHEAP BUT ATTRACTIVE CLOTHES DRAW TOURISTS TO THE STALLS AT THE BEACH TOWNS.

URBAN AND RURALSCAPE

Goa is divided into two districts, north Goa comprising the *talukas* of Pernem, Bardez, Bicholim, Sattari, and Tiswadi and South Goa comprising the *talukas* of Salcete, Mormugao, Sanguem, Quepem, and Canacona. The largest urban centre in Goa is its capital Panaji, followed by the smaller towns of Margao, Ponda, and Mapusa. The rest is fairly rural and made up of villages. The population density hovers around 350 persons per square kilometre.

Panaji, as also Margao, has a character of its own and is entirely different from the cities in the rest of India. Far from being a buzzing metropolis, it is a quiet medieval town. The old quarter of Panaji or the Latin Quarter is made up of quaint squares and a maze of lanes and bylanes. There are only traces of the crowded marketplaces, footpath hawkers, and garbage dumps associated with most state capitals, in the newer part of Panaji.

The landmark in the Latin Quarter is the church of Our Lady of Immaculate Conception. The gleaming white façade of the church, with its grand flight of stairs, towers above the municipal square. Just beyond the church is Fontainhas, Panaji's oldest residential quarter, evocative of Portuguese colonial rule. Fontainhas is between Rua de Ourem and Altinho hill. Walking around the area with its distinct Mediterranean flavour, one encounters the characteristic double storeyed houses painted in gay colours. The windows are outlined in a white band, and balconies are enclosed with wrought iron grills. Red tiled roofs and window boxes with flowers in a riot of colours complete the pretty picture.

Dotting the lanes and bylanes are a number of pubs and *tavernas* where one can

GETTING A
REJUVENATING
MASSAGE ON THE
SILVERY, SAND STREWN
BEACH.
FACING PAGE: A
TRADITIONAL
FISHERMAN, HOMEWARD
BOUND WITH FISH FOR
HIS EVENING MEAL.

saunter in for an authentic Goan meal or down a peg or two of the potent Goan *feni*. If a light snack is all you have place for, stop at the little bakeries that churn out hot breads, cakes, and patties. Almost every little street corner has a wayside cross. "If you were to drop a bomb on Goa," so goes the saying, "it would land either on a cross or on a tavern."

While Panaji is the capital and the political hub of the state, housing the Legislative Assembly, the High Court, the university and most professional colleges and institutes, Margao is the commercial hub. It is a busier town than Panaji, as it is also the nodal point and transport centre of south Goa. Margao's answer to Fontainhas is the Church of Holy Spirit Square and the Jorge Barreto Park. The focus of the town is its crowded market where every kind of Goan produce is on display from sausages made of pork, local vegetables and spices to clothes and footwear.

Rural Goa has often been described as a garland of villages, where each village is a glowing pearl. The rice fields interspersed with coconut groves form a patchwork of green-gold. Tucked away everywhere is a house. And binding them all together is the church or temple square.

Besides being a landmark of the village, the gleaming white façade of a church or temple is also the heart of the community. It serves as much for an interlude with God as for an exchange of gossip and good cheer that warms the heart. In times of sorrow, the whole village gathers around to offer sympathy and a shoulder to lean on; come joy, and the air resounds with the strains of the violin at a *ladainha*.

Goa's landed gentry, concentrated mainly in the villages, was educated in Portugal and went on to hold high posts in the administration or to become professionals. These Portuguese-speaking Christians dabbled, successfully, in trade and commerce. They built mansions for themselves on the lines of the Portuguese houses. Rarely did they migrate to the towns, preferring to lead an aristocratic lifestyle. The sale of paddy, coconuts, cashews or whatever else the land produced maintained the standard of living.

Working for the landlords were the *mundkars* or tenants-at-will. They tilled the land, looked after coconut plantations, worked as domestic helps and were generally available. In return, the landlord fed and clothed them, looked after their medical expenses and even educated or married off the offspring.

The scenario is rapidly changing. Land holdings, after they are divided between the sons, are not large enough to support a single family, leave alone joint families or tenants-at-will. The *mundkars* too, striving to better their lot, are educated and employed in towns within or outside Goa.

ARCHITECTURE

In addition to the churches and convents, the Portuguese erected several fortresses. These defended the harbour, the cities beyond and the provinces at large. These forts were garrisoned and mounted with guns, presenting an imposing aspect of Portugal's military strength. At present, most forts are in ruins.

The most important fort, due to its location, was the Fortress of Aguada. It enclosed the peninsula and formed the northern extremity of the bay at the mouth of the Mandovi river. At the summit of the hill is a citadel with a lighthouse. Within the citadel is a huge square cistern capable of holding 23,76,000 gallons of water. Built in 1612, it got its name, *Agoada* or Watering Place, since it supplied ships with water. Another fort of historical importance, the Fortress of Tiracol, was taken over from the Bhonsles in 1776.

The fortresses and the churches were the aesthetic models for civil architecture in Portuguese India. The only

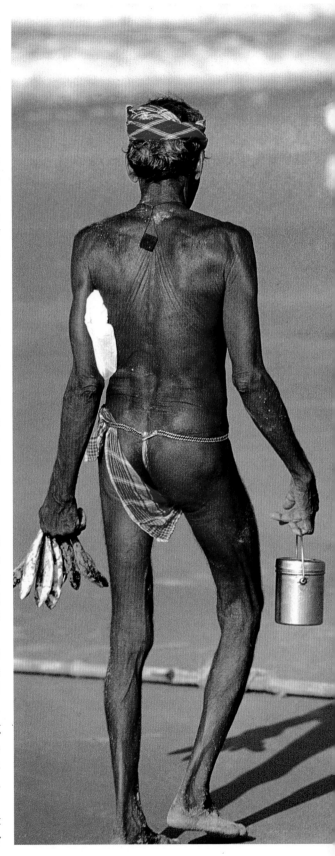

FACING PAGE: VENETIAN CUT-GLASS CHANDELIERS, GILDED MIRRORS AND BAROQUE STYLE ROSEWOOD FURNITURE REFLECT THE ECLECTIC TASTES AND LIFESTYLES OF A BYGONE ERA. PAGES 52-53: GOAN VILLAGES ARE DOTTED WITH ELEGANT COLONIAL MANSIONS BUILT BY THE LANDED GENTRY IN THE 18TH–19TH CENTURY; THE FURNITURE AND INTERIOR DÉCOR ARE EUROPEAN IN FLAVOR.

palace of Goa's golden age that remains today is the Archbishop's Palace in Old Goa. Its construction began at the end of the sixteenth century. Its characteristic features are the porch with a roof, supported on masonry columns, and a grand flight of steps. Large windows on the first floor and the smaller openings on the ground floor are highlighted with a simple surrounding plaster band. These windows with square lintels and mother-of-pearl shell shutters open onto a little corbel balcony encircled by a wooden railing. The aesthetic conveyed by the palace and other structures of the period is one of calm, solid, and imposing strength.

The houses the Goans built in the eighteenth and nineteenth centuries were modelled on the houses the Portuguese built. The houses were initially double-storeyed. Reception rooms were on the top floors; the lower floors were reserved for servants. The top floor would have a reception room or hall, a formal dining room, sleeping quarters, and sometimes a chapel, library, and study. These were grand houses with a row of windows opening onto little balconies and high, pyramidal tiled roofs. In the absence of glass, window shutters were fitted with square bits of translucent nacre from oyster shells. In the interior there were marble floors, wood panelled false ceilings, and frescoes on the walls. The houses were furnished with chandeliers, tapestry, carved furniture and rugs—all imported to suit the family's taste. China porcelain and cutlery often bore the family crest.

The houses built in the later half of the nineteenth and the early twentieth centuries were not as large. But, they were raised on a high plinth and incorporated the *balcao* (a colonnaded porch) at the entrance. The rooms became smaller. The detailing and intricacy of individual elements was enhanced. Doors and window shutters, false ceilings, wooden pillars, and railings became grander and intricate. Local craftsmen, with their own repertoire of Indian motifs, were making furniture that was, earlier, imported. The houses were as lovely as before, but more modest.

The Goan Identity

FACING PAGE: GOANS
ARE NOTED FOR THEIR
JOIE DE VIVRE AND,
GIVEN HALF A CHANCE,
BREAK INTO SONG AND
DANCE.

The glory of *Goa Dourada*, Rome of the East, does not lie merely in Goa's breathtaking scenery, its sacred shrines, and buildings. Its people, whose culture and habits have evolved over centuries, are also a part of it. Yet, are Goans westernized? What is the identity that every Goan is so proud of? What is it that sets him apart from the rest?

Goa's rich heritage is the result of an East-West amalgamation. The impact of 450 years of Portuguese colonial rule is seen in every aspect of Goan life. Today, Portuguese influence can be tasted in the food and seen in the dresses and the gay Mediterranean colours of the houses. More than anything, it is visible in the *joie de vivre* of the people.

The people who qualify as Goans are over a million. They are a social and cultural phenomenon that make for interesting study. While Goa is a state of the Indian Union, the people have no obvious claim to the country's culture. Goans are recognizable at sight as Indians, but their cultural characteristics are different.

The cultural conditioning of the Goans is due to political and religious events. These have produced a fusion of cultures rarely found elsewhere. Half the Goan female population is attired in the sari. Others, after their brush with Christianity, have adopted the western skirt, while the males wear trousers. Widows use black as a sign of mourning, rather than white which is the practice elsewhere.

The easy-going nature of the inhabitants is reflected in the gently swaying palm trees and the undulating sand dunes. It creates an impression of lethargy and has often been mistaken for laziness. But, give the Goans an occasion and they promptly break into song and dance.

There are a couple of Goan characteristics, the flip side of the *susegad* (relaxed) nature, which are often irritating. One is their scant regard for time. Lack of punctuality should never be perceived as a personal insult in Goa. There it is customary to fix an appointment for the morning and turn up at 12.00 noon.

The Goans are a mild-mannered, warm, hospitable race. The accepted form of greeting is a kiss on each cheek. They have an innate sense of politeness, a quality they admire in others. The family is the heart of every household. It is not unusual to find three generations living under one roof. Girls and boys live with the family even after they start working, moving out only after marriage. In the last century, it was fairly common to find spinster aunts and bachelor uncles living as cherished members of a household. That has slowly changed with the emergence of the nuclear family. The size of the family has greatly shrunk. Where couples earlier had an average of four / five children, sometimes going up to eight and even ten children, they now restrict themselves to two or three. Children are a part of any festivity as they are in other parts of India, unlike more formal European cultures.

FACING PAGE: GOA'S
LIVELY VILLAGE
MARKETS, WHERE
FRESH PRODUCE IS
SOLD EARLY IN THE
MORNINGS.

Goa has produced intellectually, professionally, culturally, and spiritually, an amazing race of people. Many have gained repute in medicine, engineering, literature, and the arts. The literacy level in Goa is well above the national average.

Hinduism is the religion of more than half the population of Goa, while Christianity is followed by nearly forty per cent of the population. The Muslim presence is negligible, not more than five per cent of the population. Christianity is more a way of life. It is still coloured by Hindu rituals. Fairs, festivals, and processions are a part of it. Church attendance is seen as a social occasion. Everyone turns out in their Sunday best and meets after the service to exchange news and gossip.

LANGUAGES OF THE PEOPLE

English is spoken and understood all over the state. It is the medium of instruction in schools. Though Hindi is the national language, it is hardly spoken. An influx of migrant labour has made Hindi more popular. As a result of Goa's colonial past, Portuguese was spoken by a large segment of the converts. Till today, especially, in the Latin pockets of Goa, Portuguese is spoken or understood by many Goans.

Konkani, the local language is also spoken all along the Konkan coast. The language does not have its own script and is written in the Roman, Devnagiri, Kannada, and Malayalam scripts. It imbibes the accent and vocabulary peculiar to the state or region where it is spoken. While it is not a fully developed language like Hindi or Marathi, it is more developed than a dialect. Journey from one corner of Goa to the other and you will encounter at least a dozen different dialects of Konkani. The people of south Goa can be distinguished from those of north Goa by the different ways in which they speak Konkani.

The reason that Konkani never really developed as a language is that it was used only for oral communication. In pre-Portuguese Goa, Marathi was used for written communication. During the Portuguese regime, the new converts used Portuguese while the Hindus continued using Marathi. Father Diogo Ribeiro studied the language and compiled the first grammar textbook in Konkani. Eminent linguist Mgsr Sebastian Dalgado can be credited with compiling the first Konkani-Portuguese dictionary in 1893. Much later he also wrote a Konkani grammar. But his most valuable contribution to the language is an anthology of Konkani proverbs. Konkani was granted official language status in 1987.

FOOD

The sea-washed, sun-drenched land of Goa has unsurpassed culinary skills. Goan cooks are reputed the world over and are employed aboard cruise liners and in five-star hotels. Elsi Maciel, a culinary expert, published a Goan cookery book in London in the early '80s. It was the first Asian recipe publication in the United Kingdom. Goan recipe books must now grace many European kitchen shelves.

The staple food of the Goans like that in any other place along the Konkan coast, is fish, rice, and curry. Goans are partial to tainted brown rice, which is had with spicy coconut curry and the inevitable fried fish. Fish, besides being the main dish of the daily meal, is an important ingredient of Goan life. Meet a neighbour early in the morning and the conversation starts with 'What fish have you bought today?' Men

buy fish daily for the household. Fishermen's wives line up in markets with their wares: mackerels, sardines, kingfish, pomfrets, Indian salmon, shark, mullet, mussels, crabs, prawns . . .

Fish, rice, and curry as a staple diet is common to Hindus and Catholics. The similarity in the food habits of the two communities, however, ends here. The Hindus ate fish, rice, and curry before the advent of the Portuguese and still do so. Portuguese cuisine influenced none of their other dishes. Popular snacks churned out in a Goan-Hindu kitchen are wades (puris) and deep fried onions or potatoes dipped in gram flour batter. Vegetable dishes range from banana flowers cooked in chickpeas, green bananas to alsande (a variety of beans). Every meal comes with sole khadi, a digestive, diluted juice of the cocum fruit mixed with coconut milk.

A different sweetmeat marks each of the Hindu festivals. Ganesh Chaturthi (a harvest festival) is celebrated with patolyo (rice and jaggery dumplings) and neurios (a deep fried dumpling stuffed with sweetened grated coconut), Diwali with laddoos, chaklis (a crunchy savoury) and flattened rice cooked in jaggery. The Hindu converts have incorporated beef and pork, taboo for Hindus, in their cuisine.

After the Portuguese came, the food of the Christians changed. A unique range of dishes like the mouth-watering sorpotel, caldin, xacuti, samarachi kodi, and recheado fish came up. Goan Catholic cuisine is special and different from the rest of the Konkan region. Fish, curry, and rice remains the daily fare. But the fish is often fried with a tinge of recheado masala (red chillies and spices ground in vinegar), with its unique tangy flavour.

A gathering invited for a special occasion would first be served appetisers like empadinhas (small pork pies made of rice batter) or fofo-de bacaliao (cod baked in a light pastry). Soup would inevitably follow. Either a caldo verde (spinach and potato broth) or sopa grosa. The banquet laid out in the formal dinning room would have as the main course, fish mayonnaise, apa de camarao (spicy prawn pie in a rice batter case), mussels, crabs, oyster empada (pie), roast leitao (suckling pig stuffed with sausage, liver, heart, chillies, and spices and roasted whole), pork vindaloo (pork stew seasoned with vinegar, garlic, and spices), arross refugado (pulao) garnished with fried onions, cashew nuts, and raisins. A range of homemade pickles and preserves would accompany it. Prawn *balchao*, that graces the table on a special occasion, is the stuff to dream about long after it has been digested. It has a characteristic piquant flavour—little sweet, a little tangy. Another delightful accompaniment with any meal, one that goes particularly well with plain white rice, is the crisp, fried squid.

Goa's prized dish, the *sorpotel*, is served mainly on feast days or other special occasions like Christmas, Easter or just a family get-together. Diced pieces of liver,

WOMEN OF THE FISHING COMMUNITY TAKE THE DAY'S CATCH TO THE MARKET AND DISPLAY IT ATTRACTIVELY, HOPING FOR A GOOD PRICE.

TOP: TODAY'S SPECIAL
AT THE FISH MARKET,
THESE POMFRETS WILL
BECOME STUFFED
RECHEADO AND GRACE
THE TABLE OF A GOAN
BATCAR.
RIGHT: LED THROUGH A
SERIES OF NETS INTO A
FINAL DEATH CHAMBER.
THE CATCH RANGES
FROM POMFRETS,
MACKERELS AND
SARDINES TO SHRIMPS
AND TIGER PRAWNS.

A CAMEO BEAUTY WITH
A GORGEOUS MANE OF
HAIR.
FACING PAGE:
COLOURFUL WEEKLY
MARKETS WHERE THE
TANTALIZING AROMA OF
LOCAL PRODUCTS
DRAWS SHOPPERS.

heart, and kidney are first fried and then cooked in deliciously thick gravy (often thickened with pig's blood). *Sorpotel* is usually accompanied with *sannas*, steamed coconut rice cakes that have a hint of toddy in place of yeast. Another pride of Goan cuisine is its sausage. Pickled pieces of pork are stuffed in gut and sun-dried. *Choricio pao*, the Goan sausage, stuffed in bread is a favourite any-time snack.

Of the chicken dishes, *xacuti* and *cafreal*, vie with each other for a place on the list of top ten Goan dishes. Chicken *xacuti* has chicken pieces marinated in a gravy made up of green *masala* and finely grated bits of coconut cooked in coconut milk. Chicken *cafreal* is grilled chicken marinated in a generous quantity of garlic paste and served with salad.

Greens and vegetables somehow get sidetracked in a Goan kitchen. Adding dried shrimps or prawn spices up an obligatory dish of ladyfinger or pumpkin.

Of the desserts, *bebinca* is a not-to-miss experience. It is a rich, eight-layered cake made from egg yolks, coconut milk, and sugar and is the grand finale to any Goan banquet. A range of sweets is made at Christmas. A must-eat is the Christmas cake made with dried fruit, nuts, rum, etc. Other sweets range from milk toffee, fudge, marzipan, macaroons, *doce de grao*, *batica* (coconut and semolina cake), *dodol*, *kokada*, *bolinas*, and *neurios*.

The ingredients common to most of these dishes which give the food its unique flavour are red chillies, coconut jaggery, vinegar made from toddy, garlic, ginger, pepper, cloves, cumin, cinnamon and, of course, grated coconut. Chillies and vinegar are perhaps the most vital ingredients. Vinegar imparts the tangy flavour that is missing in Goan Hindu food. The Portuguese introduced chillies into Goa from their colony in Brazil.

The Portuguese also perfected the art of making vinegar from coconut toddy. The toddy is left to ferment and then put in an earthen pot with a roof tile that has been heated till it is red-hot. The chemical reaction caused by the roof tile produces bacteria that give vinegar its flavour.

No trip to Goa is complete without sampling these culinary delights at one of the beach shacks or totting up on Goa's local brew, *feni*. Sitting at a shack with a plate of *masala* fried prawns at your elbow and sipping a pint of beer as you watch the sun disappear over the horizon is the ultimate Goan experience.

Goa's famous *feni* is now finding favour with connoisseurs all over India and even abroad. Every tourist who returns from Goa is sure to take back a bottle or two of *feni*. The fact that it is very cheap has also popularised the local brew. As *feni* is considered to be country liquor, it cannot be sold anywhere else in India. Envisaging the great export potential of *feni*, efforts are being made to register it internationally on the basis of the Geographical Indication Bill under the Lisbon agreement of the World Intellectual Property Rights Association.

There are two types of *feni*, the cashew *feni* and the coconut *feni*. The aroma of this ethnic, exotic white spirit is an integral part of enjoying a drink. Goans generally prefer it undiluted or mixed with soda. While the *feni* has a very distinct flavour it is also versatile enough to be used as a base for cocktails.

The traditional method of making *feni* is called the potstill method. Cashew *feni* is distilled from the juice of the cashew fruit, which was introduced into Goa from Brazil by the Portuguese. Coconut *feni* is distilled from the toddy collected from coconut trees. In the traditional potstill method, a circular copper or earthen pot

BEMUSED TOURISTS
WATCH GYPSIES WITH
THEIR BAND OF
PERFORMERS.

containing fermented cashew juice or coconut toddy is heated by placing it over a flame or by injecting steam. The vapours of alcohol rise through the swan-like neck of the vessel and are collected as a liquid after they pass through a water-cooled condenser. The first distillate thus obtained is called *urack* and it is a light, refreshing summer drink. This low strength *urack* is further distilled, matured, and sometimes blended to get the potent drink called *feni*.

ART OF LIVING

Nowhere else in India does rural aristocracy display the level of sophistication that is seen in the villages of Goa. You drive through narrow, winding village roads, traverse large house-less stretches, seeing only miles and miles of paddy fields, coconut plantations, and fruit orchards. Turn the next corner and you encounter a little village square with a white gleaming church standing out like a beacon amid a cluster of palatial homes. Enter a mansion and you are greeted either in Portuguese or strongly accented English. Warmth and hospitality are much in evidence as you are invited into a hall decorated with Belgian mirrors, chandeliers, and carved rosewood furniture. You are offered tea with dainty cakes or sandwiches in delicate Chinese porcelain, replete with tea serviettes. If you have managed to strike a cordial note with the hostess, she will even entertain you with a piece of Chopin or Mozart on the piano prominently placed in the room. This finesse in a rural setting was what you least expected when you walked towards the house, negotiating grazing fowl and a pig or two scurrying for cover.

Nothing changed the lifestyle of Goans as much as conversion to Christianity. Till the eighteenth century the average Goan, like any other person along the Konkan, built his home around a quadrangle that was divided internally with the bare minimum number of partitions. As personal fortunes improved, features like a porch and rear veranda were added. According to historical research on the subject, until the eighteenth century the local population (the Hindus and the Christians) had not assimilated Portuguese culture and taste.

It was only after the eighteenth century that a synthesis between the East and the West was reflected in the Goans' cultural life. Its manifestation is most vibrant in the houses built then in Goa. The *balcao* is the airy reception room, where the family spent its leisure time and neighbours sat together. Gossip coloured the evenings and laughter and song lightened the air after a hard day's toil. The *balcao* opens into a little *saletta,* or parlour, off which is a large formal *sala.* The *sala* is the main reception room. Wealth and attention was lavished on these halls to make them a fitting background for formal entertaining. The family received their guests under handmade chandeliers to the accompaniment of music. Family portraits adorned the walls, and silk, brocade, and lace curtains fluttered in the window openings. Beautifully carved furniture was sometimes custom-made. A common feature is the incorporation of a family shrine or chapel, often in a separate room dedicated to worship. Some houses have modest altars whereas others have grand chapels, but all houses contain some form of an oratory, which was the heart of the family. Many chapels are of a splendour comparable if not superseding that of the rest of the house. The richly carved altars house beautifully painted ivory and wood statues, icons and silver candlesticks. The *retables* are often decorated with religious motifs.

In a Hindu household, food was served on banana fronds and people ate sitting on mats or on the floor. It was usual to have the men eat first, followed by the children, and then the women. In the Catholic house, the concept of a separate dining room was imbibed from the Portuguese. People now dined seated on chairs. The room had as much attention bestowed on it as the *sala.* The intricately carved dining chairs often had the coat of arms carved on their backs. Console tables, heavily carved, would be placed around in lieu of a sideboard.

In the traditional Hindu household, women and children slept together on the floor on mats and the men slept together in a separate space also on the floor or on a *khat.* The Catholic houses, however, paid attention to the bedrooms. One of the larger bedrooms in the house was reserved for the master of the house. The bedroom almost always had a false ceiling, panelled, and with elaborate designs. The room was elegantly appointed with a large carved bed in rosewood or mahogany. The other pieces of furniture in the room—the washbasin stand, writing desk, and dressing table—were all co-ordinated pieces with the same motif carved on each.

THERE IS ALMOST NO LIMIT TO THE VARIETY OF WATER SPORTS OFFERED. PARASAILING, WINDSURFING, JET SKIING, BUMP RIDES AND WATER SCOOTERS ARE ALL THE RAGE. PAGES 66-67: THE SEA GLISTENING IN THE SUN, STRETCHES OF GOLDEN SAND AND A WHISPERING OF PALMS—ALL CONJURE UP THE IDYLLIC HOLIDAY AMBIENCE.

Joie De Vivre

'If music be the food of life, play on,' wrote the Bard. The Goans took him very seriously. Music flows in every Goan's blood. Almost every second person strums a guitar, plays the piano, violin and mandolin or, if all else fails, can sing like a lark. Music, dance, and drama have been intricately woven with religious activities even before the arrival of the Portuguese. Traditionally, *bhajans* and *kirtans* (devotional songs) were sung daily in temples. Festivals were celebrated with devotees chanting and moving to the rhythm of drumbeats. As the beat quickened, the dancing would reach a feverish pitch with a single drumbeat signalling the end of the dance. A troupe of *devadasis*, literally Wives of Gods, performed the temple dances. The harmonium, *tabla*, and other percussion instruments accompanied the singers and dancers.

After the Portuguese arrived, the cultural amalgamation turned into a mellower mix of music and drama. The contents of the new religion were dramatized for the Hindus. Novices were made to sing the catechism or prayers. The Passion of Christ during Lent was dramatized along the streets. Even today visitors can witness *Santos Passos*, the Passion Show, which covers Christ's progress to the Crucifixion. It has a life-size image of Christ carrying the cross and is set to music.

Another traditional form of musical devotion, a legacy left behind by the Portuguese, is the *ladainhas*. These are litanies praising Mother Mary. They are sung for nine consecutive days. On the last day, everyone is invited to partake of the *prasad*, which takes the form of boiled gram accompanied, of course, by a tot of *feni*.

Goa's traditional music consists of *mandos*, *dulpods,* and *fados*. In a broad sense, the *Mando* is regarded as the Goan anthem. While it was conceived in the houses of the landed gentry, it is classical and cannot be termed folk music. It traversed all social barriers to become a common medium for appreciating the finer sentiments of life. Briefly, a *mando* is a story told with economy. The words hint at the message rather than express it fully. Sometimes it's a mellow love song; at other times, it speaks of sweet sorrow or despair. Poverty is expressed vividly. The essence of the *mando* lies as much in its contents as its melody. To the western ear, the *mando* is full-bodied Oriental music replete with a prolonged, languid, slumbering tone. To the eastern ear, it appears strange and western. The *mando* expresses Goan individuality. It takes a true Goan to understand the notes that change rapidly from a minor to a major key. The melody spins a web; the incantation and the words are pure magic.

And where there is sublime music for the soul, the body responds. The *mando* is inevitably accompanied by dance. A row of women stands facing a row of men. The women holding fans in their hands epitomize femininity; the men with kerchiefs held by their finger tips articulate the sensuousness of romance. As the story begins the

FACING PAGE:
FESTIVALS IN GOA
ARE NOTED FOR THEIR
COLOUR, MUSIC, AND
DRAMA.

dancers sway to the rhythm, absorbed in the tale. As the story unfolds, the dance rises to a crescendo. The hilarity and heartiness of its grand finale take the *mando* from the realms of classical music into the corridors of folk music.

Dulpods are fast-paced pieces, which are a sequel to *mandos*. Invariably, *dulpods* portray Goan life and its share of human foibles. The *fado* is the endangered one among the three forms. It is traditional, native Portuguese music that expresses *saudade*. Simply described, *saudade* is an aching, ethereal melancholy or a yearning for something lost or unattainable. Reggae, techno and rap have taken over from *mandos*, *dulpods,* and *fados*.

Tiatr is a century-old folk art synonymous with Goa. *Tiatrs* started off being an integral part of the numerous church and chapel festivities in villages. Their popularity grew. Today, performances are held in auditoriums in cities. Most Goans delight in these theatrical productions in Konkani that have ironic portraits of village personalities, like the parish priest, local landlord, village siren or drunk. The uniqueness of the *tiatr* lies in each act being interspersed with topical songs.

The scriptwriters produce stories that pull at one's heartstrings and have juicy dialogues. Some themes, dramatised to good effect, highlight fidelity as the hallmark of marriage. Others drive home the message that a craving for money rather than love can prove disastrous. The ever-popular stories are woven around man's insatiable greed. Some enterprising directors have tried to handle unusual topics like women caught in prostitution, etc. The most popular among the cast are the comedians. Each *tiatr* is sure to have either a *paan*-spitting villain, a simpleton with a strange accent or a stammering fool. The musical essence of the *tiatr* is the live band replete with a saxophone and trumpets. One shudders to think that the curtain may come down on it, with electronic gadgetry replacing the live band and actors moving off Goa in search of greener pastures.

FESTIVALS OF THE SPIRIT

Festivals in Goa are noted for their colour, music, and drama. Be it a religious festival like Christmas or Ganesh Chaturthi, each has unique traditions and rituals kept alive and handed down the generations. Each community has its religious festivals, but some festivals like Carnival and Shigmo have become fairly universal; the Hindus and Catholics participating with equal enthusiasm.

The festival in Goa that has gained maximum publicity is Carnival. Given its merry nature and the fact that it is unheard of anywhere else on the continent, it draws hordes. The word carnival is derived from the Latin word *carne* meaning meat, and *vale*, which translates to good-bye. It refers to the abstinence observed by Catholics during the forty-day

period of Lent. Before Lent, which is marked by Ash Wednesday, comes Carnival. It heralds three days of feasting.

Originally, Carnival was celebrated in Goan villages with an indigenous flavour. Though celebrated by the Christians, Carnival's only relevance to Christianity is that it is celebrated before Lent. Groups of village youth go around the village, throwing water and talcum powder on everyone. Some would be in fancy dress; others would enact a short skit at the doorstep.

Today, the festival, which falls in February–March, has been commercialized. Each village and corporate house prepares colourful floats, depicting popular songs and themes. They are taken in a procession through Panaji's streets and judged on originality and the revellers' musical abilities. Street dances, cultural functions and competitions abound. King Momo, the Carnival mascot, declares the festival open and gives his subjects the liberty to make merry for three days.

Shigmo is Goa's version of Holi, the ancient Hindu spring festival. Today, like Carnival, Shigmo has become commercialized, with floats winding through Panaji. The parades are a fairly authentic display of Hindu mythology and ethnicity. Themes like the Maratha conquest of Goa are used in floats. Kunbi folk dances and other

THE FUN TIMES ROLL FOR THREE CONSECUTIVE DAYS DURING CARNIVAL. PAGE 72: AN EAST-WEST AMALGAMATION IS SEEN IN EVERY ASPECT OF GOAN LIFE. PAGE 73: ORIGINALLY, CARNIVAL WAS CELEBRATED WITH AN INDIGENOUS FLAVOUR, WITH THE YOUTH GOING FROM DOOR TO DOOR ENACTING A SHORT SKIT.

THE ENTIRE VILLAGE IS
OUT ON THE STREETS TO
EITHER PARTICIPATE IN
OR MERELY WATCH THE
CARNIVAL REVELRY.
FACING PAGE: DANCES,
STREET PLAYS AND
CONTESTS COMMENCE
AFTER KING MOMO
DECLARES THE
FESTIVITIES OPEN.

Goan regional dances, performed with costumes and full gear, are a colourful spectacle. The acrobats, fire-throwers, men marching with poles to the beat of the drums, others dancing with decorated umbrellas, all provide entertainment.

Catholic festivals are usually celebrated on a fixed day every year except for Easter and the related celebrations that change yearly. All such festivals are a result of the conversion to Christianity and, therefore, show a strong Portuguese influence.

Easter that falls in March or April and Christmas (25 December) are celebrated in all churches across Goa with special mass and prayer services. Associated with Easter are the bunny and Easter eggs, exchanged between families and friends. Christmas tends to be a longer celebration. A family will start preparations a few days before Christmas, with a crib depicting the nativity tableau. A star symbolising the Star of David is hung outside each house, and a Christmas tree erected. Sweetmeats are sent across. On X-mas Day itself, it is normal to visit friends and family and partake of wine and Christmas cake together. All over the state, both on Easter Eve and Christmas Eve, street dances are held with live bands. The dancing goes on till the early morning hours.

Each village church celebrates the feast day of its patron saint. A special mass with a choir is held in the morning followed by a fete in the church grounds. The evening entertainment takes the form of a Konkani *tiatr*. The popular church feast

is the feast of Our Lady of Immaculate Conception celebrated on 8 December in Panaji with a week-long street fair.

The Church of the Holy Spirit celebrates its feast in the final days of May. In addition to mass, there is a fair scheduled prior to the onset of the rains. People come from all over Goa to buy their provisions of dry fish, household items, spices, and furniture. Besides the feasts celebrated in each village are those associated with religion, like the feast of St. Francis Xavier, the Procession of All Saints, the Feast of the Passion of Christ and the Harvest Festival.

The Procession of All Saints is celebrated at St. Andrew's Church, Goa Velha, on the Monday following Palm Sunday. The only other place that has this feast is Rome. It draws hundreds of people from neighbouring villages. After mass, celebrated in the church square to accommodate the numbers, statues of saints are taken in a procession through the streets. The life story of each saint is narrated as his statue emerges.

The Harvest Festival thanks the Almighty for a good crop. Most Goan villages celebrate it on 15 August, the feast day of Our Lady of Assumption. The few exceptions are the village of Raia that celebrates it on 5 August; Aldona, Salvador do Mundo, and Bardez celebrate it on 6 August. A statue of the Saviour of the World holding a gold sickle is taken from the church to the field opposite. The priest uses the sickle to symbolically harvest the paddy. Each church has its rituals and traditions.

The feast of St. Francis Xavier, celebrated on 3 December, draws thousands of devotees from Goa as well as other parts of the world. The great love and devotion of Goans for their *Goencho Saib* is evident in the sheer numbers that arrive to hear mass or attend the prayer services at the Basilica. During the exposition of the relics of St. Francis Xavier held every ten years, the crowds are even larger. Queues beginning at 4 a.m. continue till 8 in the evening. Preceding the solemn feast, devotees camp in the corridors of the Basilica, during the nine-day novenas.

Hindus in Goa celebrate Diwali. The focus of Diwali has shifted from the *puja* of Laxmi (Goddess of Wealth) in shops and business establishments to homes. Brightly coloured paper *akashdive* (sky-lamps) and buntings decorate the streets. Firecrackers can be heard early morning when effigies of the demon, Narkasura, are burnt to symbolize the victory of righteousness. The most significant festival of the Hindus fetes Ganesha, the elephant-headed God of learning, skill, and good fortune. Almost every Hindu Goan returns to his village ancestral house for the occasion. Months before *Ganesha Chaturthi,* terracotta artisans make clay statues of Lord Ganesha, which are painted in vibrant colours. It is very much a family festival with sweets like *neurios* (sweet puffs) and *laddoos* being given to friends and relatives.

Every temple has its annual *yatra*, when the temple deity is taken through the

village in an ornate chariot. A cacophonic band is an integral part of the procession as it meanders through streets lined with people. Of all the *yatras* held, the May one in the small town of Shirgao is exceptional. Thousands of devotees of Lairai gather and for the entire day undertake rituals and *poojas* culminating in a walk through hot coals raked from an enormous bonfire. Men and women bathe in tanks near the temple after which the devotees walk barefoot to the temple hill as an act of penance, endurance, and worship. At 10 p.m., the temple dance starts in front of the image of Lairai. Around midnight, the dancing ceases and a massive bonfire is lit. The devotees, sticks in hand, chant round the bonfire. In the early morning, when the fire dies down, the coals are raked and the anticipated ritual begins. One by one and in quick succession, the devotees run through the hot coals carrying their stick and screaming 'Lairai'—a spectacle definitely worth watching.

THE YOUNG AND THE OLD, MALE AND FEMALE ALL JOIN IN DURING CARNIVAL; THERE IS NO BAR ON ANY CASTE, CREED OR SEX FROM HAVING FUN.
FACING PAGE: A YOUNG MAN BALANCES A TRAY WITH GREAT EASE AS HE PEDALS FORTH ON A BICYCLE.

FACING PAGE:
A YOUNG MAN
BALANCES A TRAY
WITH GREAT EASE AS
HE PEDALS FORTH
ON A BICYCLE.

SPORTS

Being branded *susegad*, one would assume Goans spend every spare moment either lazing beneath a swaying palm or strolling along the beach. Engaging in physical activity or sports, one would assume, is too much to expect from a Goan. That would be quite wrong. While cricket has gained a following recently, football has always been the Goan's first love, with hockey being the second. The Portuguese introduced football (but not the obsession for it) into Goa. Come rain or sunshine, a group can be seen kicking a ball after the day's toil is over.

Football first arrived in Goa in 1883. The Goan Football Association, set up in 1959, has been conducting regular league matches. Goa was the first state to introduce professional football in the country. The football season starts from October and continues till February–March. Matches are held all over and draw a crowd. Finals of important matches become social events with bands, food stalls, alcohol, and a rowdy game of *tambola* thrown in at half time.

Another sport that is a remnant of the Portuguese era is bullfighting—with a difference. In Portugal, the show of strength is between a matador and a bull; in Goa, bulls fight each other. Compared to Portugal, where the anxiety is reserved for the matador, sequinned and rakish; here the cheering is for the bulls alone. Unlike Portugal where the bullfights are held in an indoor stadium, the arena here is in the open air, with no fences or barricades. Bullfights are usually held in a paddy field just outside a village. The pushing, straining crowd acts as a fence and enclosure.

It takes months of training and a precisely monitored diet with vitamin supplements to get a bull ready to face another. The charm of the bullfight is, of course, the heavy betting. The fights are advertised on the sports pages of the local dailies. What cannot escape your attention are the quixotic names given to the bulls: Alibaba, Second Krishna, Mad Max, Sea Harrier, and King of South are some.

To keep pace with changing trends the world over, Goa has taken steps to promote adventure sports to attract tourists. Water sports ranging from windsurfing, scuba diving, and snorkelling to water skiing have been introduced along with the five-star hotel culture. Other adventure sports like parasailing and paragliding have also been introduced.

> In short, it is easy to see why most Goans turn nostalgic at the mere mention of their homeland, Goa. Just whisper the word and the ears prick up, the eyes turn dewy and a kaleidoscope of images flashes through the mind's eye . . . the little hamlet surrounded by the lush countryside, evenings spent out on the *balcao* strumming a guitar while sipping a glass of *feni,* the anticipation of *sannas* dipped in *sorpotel* . . .

All rights are reserved. No part of this
publication may be transmitted or reproduced
in any form or by any means without prior
permission from the publisher.

ISBN: 81-7436-284-3

© Roli & Janssen BV 2004
Published in India by
Roli Books in arrangement with
Roli & Janssen BV, The Netherlands
M-75, Greater Kailash II Market
New Delhi-110 048, India.
Ph: ++91 (11) 29210886, 29212782, 29212271
Fax: ++91 (11) 29217185
Email: roli@vsnl.com; Website: rolibooks.com

PHOTO CREDITS

Amit Pasricha
2-3, 4, 5, 8, 9, 12, 13, 14-15, 16-17, 19, 22-23, 24, 26, 27
28-29, 34, 37, 44-45 (one pix), 51, 52-53, 54, 57, 58-59
60, 61, 62, 66-67, 68, 70, 71, 72, 73, 74, 76-77

Thomas Kelly
Front cover, back cover, 11, 20-21, 30 (both), 31, 32, 33, 35
38-39, 40, 42-43, 45, 46, 47, 49, 63, 64, 78

Pallava Bagla
1, 6-7, 48, 65

Roli Collection
75

Printed and bound at Singapore